Diet recommendations for TCM - Large intestine - dryness of the colon

Please check these recommendations always with a TCM nutrition consultant, therapist, doctor or dietician. The recipes and the list of ingredients are supporting also the conventional medical therapy. The calorie disclosures of fresh ingredients (fruit and vegetables) vary according to quality and time of harvest. The contents were checked by a dietician and a nutrition consultant for the Traditional Chinese Medicine (TCM).

Author:
©2017 Josef Miligui
www.ebns.at

AF236105

Source:
The lists are created from the EBNS database for nutritional counseling. The database is used by dietitians, therapists and doctors for advising the patient / client.

Literature:
The specialist literature and the training documents of the German and Austrian dietary and traditional Chinese medicine serve as a knowledge base. We have used the documents as a basis of knowledge, adapted it to our experience and completed them.
http://di-book.com

Title Photo:
©2008 Erika Weixlbaumer

Production and publishing:
BoD – Books on Demand, Norderstedt
ISBN: 9783752855265

Diet recommendations for TCM - Large intestine - dryness of the colon

1   Treatment strategy

Promote body fluids, reduce heat, moisturize dryness, promote bowel movements.

2   Avoid

n.a.

3   Breakfast

	kkal. per serving
Black beans with avocado	263
Bulgur with tomatoes and fresh herbs	205
Cherry cereal porridge - also for babies from the 8th month	219
Cooling rice dish with grapefruit	234
Cous-Cous with date, coco and almondpuree	483
Italian champignon rice	256
Millet with egg and butter	338
Polenta with peach	197
Polenta with ratatouille	225
Quick flakes with compote or jam	189

4   Snack

5   Lunch

6   Afternoon

7 Dinner

8 Any time

9 Recipes

9.1 8 treasures of rice

Strengthens kidney and bladder, builds up Qi, strengthens the spleen, repels moisture, reduces internal heat, prevents cancer, builds heart, calms nerves.
Cooking time approx. 1 hour
Calories p. portion: 212
4 portions

Quantity of ingredients
Lily bulbs 1 table spoon / 5g. .... *
Longane 1 table spoon / 5g. .... *
King Solomon's-seal 1 table spoon / 5g. .... *
Yam root, yam root tuber 1 table spoon / 5g. .... *
Coix (seeds) YiYi Ren 1 table spoon / 5g. .... *
Rice wild (nature rice) 1 1/2 cups / 240g. .... metal
Water 8-10 cups / 800g. (yes) .... earth

Cooking instructions:
Each one 1 tbsp: Bai He, Longan, Yu Zhu, Da Zao, Shan Yao, Lian Mi, Yi Yi Ren, Qian Shi
Add hot water and soak for about 30 minutes. Then add 1 - 2 cups of rice (normal) and simmer for 1/2 to 1 hour until the rice is very soft. Or: Cook for about 3 hours with the herbs a congee. Then the herbs do not have to be soaked.

9.2 Basic recipe for a beef broth (clear)

Strengthens Qi and Yang, is very warming.
Cooking time approx. 4-8 hours
Calories p. portion: 114
10 portions
Allergens: O

Quantity of ingredients
Beef soup meat 1,1 lbs / 500g. .... earth
Beef meatbones 5/8 oz / 200g. .... earth
Vinegar (Red wine vinegar) 1 dash / 3g. .... wood
Juniper berry 8 pieces / 6g. .... fire
Rosemary 1 pinch / 1g. .... fire
Carrot 3 pieces / 210g. .... earth

Parsnip 2 pieces / 300g. .... fire
Leek 1 piece / 200g. .... metal
Ginger fresh 1/2 teaspoon / 5g. .... metal
Lovage 1 stem / 15g. .... metal
Clove 2 pieces / 2g. .... metal
Pimento 6 pieces / 12g. .... metal
Anise (Common Fennel) 2 pieces / 1g. .... earth
Salt 1 teaspoon / 5g. .... water
Water 3,3 lbs / 1300g. .... earth

Cooking instructions:
Heat water, a dash of red wine vinegar, some juniper berries, a little
rosemary, bones and meat till it boils; add carrot, parsnip, leek, ginger,
lovage, clove, allspice, star anise and a little salt; simmer for 4-8 hours
then strain.
Refrigerate for later use.

9.3   Basic recipe for a chicken broth worming

Strengthens Qi and blood, is very warm.
Cooking time approx. 2-3 hours
Calories p. portion: 90
9 portions
Allergens: L

Quantity of ingredients
Chicken meat 1/2 piece / 600g. .... wood
Carrot 2 pieces / 150g. .... earth
Leek 1 stick / 45g. .... metal
Celery root 1 piece / 500g. .... earth
Ginger fresh 2 slices / 2g. .... metal
Fenugreek (Trigonella foenum-graecum) 1 teaspoon / 2g. .... *
Juniper berry 1 teaspoon / 3g. .... fire
Bay leaf 3 pieces / 2g. .... *
Water 4 cup / 900g. .... earth

Cooking instructions:
Remove chicken parts from fat. Place chicken pieces in a saucepan with
hot water and heat till it boils briefly, skimming any resulting foam. Add
coarsely chopped vegetables and all spices and cook over medium heat
for 2 to 3 hours. Strain the finished soup. Throw away vegetables and
bones.
Tip: If you want to use the meat as a soup insert, take out after 45

minutes and return only the bones in the soup.
Refrigerate for later use.

9.4 Basic recipe for a fish broth

Strengthens kidney Qi and Yin, strengthens blood and fluids, promotes urination.
Cooking time approx. 40 min
Calories p. portion: 128
5 portions
Allergens: DLO

Quantity of ingredients
Fish pieces mixed (fresh water) 3/4 lbs / 300g. ....water
Celery root 1/4 lbs - 4oz / 120g. .... earth
Leek 2 inches / 10g. ....metal
Carrot 2 pieces / 150g. .... earth
White wine 1/2 cup / 125g. ....wood
Lemon 1/2 piece / 50g. ....wood
Bay leaf 2 leaves / 2g. ....*
Peppercorns 3 pieces / 2g. ....metal
Olive oil 1 table spoon / 10g. .... earth
Water 2 cup / 450g. .... earth

Cooking instructions:
Fry celery, chopped carrots and leeks in olive oil, add bay leaf and peppercorns, add pieces of fish and sauté briefly. Add water, add little white wine or lemon. Simmer gently for 30 minutes. Skim off the resulting foam several times. In the end, sift the ingredients through a cloth. Refrigerate for later use.

9.5 Beetroot soup

Dissolves stagnation, relaxes, builds up Qi.
Cooking time approx. 20-30 min
Calories p. portion: 282
4 portions
Allergens: G

Quantity of ingredients
Olive oil 2 table spoons / 20g. .... earth
Onion white 1 piece chopped / 50g. ....metal
Garlic 1 clove / 2g. ....metal
Red beet 2,2 lbs (Peeled and diced) / 1000g. .... earth

Cumin (Caraway seed) 1 table spoon / 7g. ....metal
Curcuma 1 teaspoon / 2g. .... *
Oregano fresh 1 pinch of fresh / 2g. ....metal
Peppers (rose peppers) 1 teaspoon / 2g. .... earth
Créme fraiche cheese 1/4 lbs - 4oz / 125g. .... *

Cooking instructions:
Heat the oil in a saucepan, fry the onions and garlic in dark brown. Add cumin, turmeric, oregano and salt and deglaze with 1 liter of water. Cook the beetroot for about 20 minutes. Puree the soup and serve in soup bowls with 1 tbsp. crème fraiche. Finally, sprinkle the rose pepper over it.

9.6   Black beans with avocado

Nourishing and slightly refreshing, builds up fluids, filling, nourishes Yin von liver, lungs and colon, moisturizes, relaxes, builds up Qi, spreads, forces stomach and kidney.
Cooking time approx. 1 hour
Calories p. portion: 264
3 portions
Allergens: EN

Quantity of ingredients
Black beans 1 cup / 100g. ....water
Water 4 cups / 450g. (yes) .... earth
Lemon 1 dash / 1g. ....wood
Boxhorn clover seeds 1 pinch (powder) / 0,2g. ....*
Sesame oil 1 table spoon / 10g. .... earth
Ginger fresh 1 teaspoon / 2g. ....metal
Wakame 1 inch / 1g. ....water
Soy sauce 1 dash / 1g. ....water
Avocado 1 piece / 300g. .... earth

Cooking instructions:
Preparation the day before:
Soak 2 cups of black beans in about 6 cups of cold water for 6-8 hours and then strain.
Put the black beans in 4 cups of fresh cold water; add a dash of lemon juice, some fenugreek seed powder, 1 tablespoon of sesame oil, 1 teaspoon of grated ginger; add a piece of wakame or 1 tbsp of hijiki. Simmer for about 45 minutes; puree with the blender; season with plenty of soy sauce.

In the morning: Peel ½ avocado per serving and cut into small boats; Serve with the warm bean paste.

Note: The black beans can be pre-cooked for 2 - 3 days to be used as breakfast or other meals with little effort.

9.7 Bulgur with tomatoes and fresh herbs

Very refreshing, builds up fluids.
Cooking time approx. 30 min
Calories p. portion: 205
1 portions
Allergens: A

Quantity of ingredients
Bulgur (cereals) 1 cup / 120g. .... wood
Tomato 2 pieces / 70g. .... wood
Rucola 2 table spoons / 16g. .... fire
Pepper powder (hot) 1 pinch / 2g. .... fire
Olive oil 2 table spoons / 20g. .... earth
Pepper (ground) 1 pinch / 0,5g. .... metal
Salt 1 pinch / 1g. .... water
Basil 4 leaves / 2g. .... metal
Thyme 1 Twig / 3g. .... *
Lemon juice 1/2 piece / 10g. .... wood

Cooking instructions:
Put cold water in a pot, sprinkle in Bulgur and simmer. Stir in chopped tomatoes, fresh herbs like basil, thyme, arugula, a pinch of rose paprika, lemon juice, a dash of olive oil, a little ground pepper, some salt.
Variant: add some mozzarella.
Recommendation: ideal morning meal in summer; also suitable as evening meal, especially for sleep disorders.

9.8 Carp soup

Nourishing and slightly warming, strengthens the middle and the lower heater, removes moisture.
Cooking time approx. 2 hours
Calories p. portion: 499
2 portions
Allergens: DO

Quantity of ingredients

Carp 1,1 lbs / 500g. ....water
Salt 1 pinch / 1g. ....water
Vinegar (Apple vinegar) 1 teaspoon / 3g. ....wood
Thyme 1 Twig / 3g. ....*
Juniper berry 8 pieces / 3g. .... fire
Carrot 2 pieces / 200g. .... earth
Leek 1 piece / 200g. ....metal
Onion white 1 piece / 60g. ....metal
Ginger fresh 1/2 teaspoon / 2g. ....metal
Bay leaf 3 leaves / 1g. ....*
White wine 1/2 cup / 125g. ....wood
Basil 3 leaves / 1g. ....metal

Cooking instructions:
Preparation: When shopping at the fishmonger, remove the fillets from a medium-sized, whole carp and also pack the fish head, spine with bones and tail.

Cut the fillets into 1 cm cubes; salt and set aside.

Place fish head, backbone and tail of carp in plenty of cold water; heat till it boils and scoop the foam; add a dash of vinegar, a fresh sprig of thyme, juniper berries; Add carrot, a piece of leek and chopped onion; add a thick slice of ginger, some peppercorns, 1 bay leaf, salt; simmer for about 1 1/2 hours and pour the stock through a sieve.
Put the carp pieces in a saucepan; pour a shot of white wine; Add rose paprika, basil leaves, finely ground carrots, dried thyme and the stock and warm; Boil the ingredients for about 5 minutes until the fish pieces are cooked.
Variants: Thicken the soup with kudzu or mashed potatoes.
This fits: baguette and dry white wine.

9.9   Cherry cereal porridge

Reduces internal heat, moisturizes intestines, relaxes, builds up Qi, strengthens middle, reduces internal heat, nourishes Yin from heart and kidney, preserves the fluids, strengthens heart blood.
Cooking time approx. 10 min
Calories p. portion: 219
1 portions
Allergens: AG

Quantity of ingredients

Cherry 1/8 lbs - 2oz / 50g. .... earth
Water 3/4 cup - 6 oz / 200g. (yes).. earth
Wheat flakes 1/2 oz / 20g. ....wood
Banana 1/8 lbs - 2oz / 50g. .... earth
Butter organic 1 table spoon / 10g. .... earth

Cooking instructions:

Thoroughly wash the cherries, pluck from the stems and core. Drain the cherries from the glass and defrost the frozen ones. Cook the cherries with the water and the flakes in a saucepan over low heat while stirring for about 4 minutes until the cherries are soft. Add the banana and the butter to the porridge, finely grate with the blender.

9.10 Chicken soup with angelica root and buckthorn fruit

Strengthens spleen and nourishes the blood and Yin of the liver, forces Qi and blood, is very warming.
Cooking time approx. 1 1/2 hours
Calories p. portion: 77
3 portions
Allergens: LO

Quantity of ingredients

Basic recipe for a chicken soup (warming) 2 cup / 500g. ....*
Angelica root 1/8 oz / 5g. ....*
Bocksdorn fruits, goji berry dried 1/8 lbs - 2oz / 50g. .... wood

Cooking instructions:

When you cook chicken broth according to basic recipes add angelica root and willowberry fruits in the last 40 minutes.
Ingestion: Drink 2-3 cups of broth daily.

9.11 Clear oxen tail soup with buckthorn fruit

Forces Qi, nourishes the liver blood, good for ocular fibrillation or dry eyes, muscle tension or calf cramps due to blood deficiency.
Cooking time approx. 1-2 hours
Calories p. portion: 217
6 portions
Allergens: O

Quantity of ingredients

Basic recipe for a beef soup (warming) 4 cup / 1000g. ....*
Beef Oxtail pieces 1,1 lbs / 500g. .... earth
Shiitake, dried 4-5 pieces / 4g. .... earth
Onion white 1 piece / 60g. ....metal
Sake 2 table spoons / 20g. ....metal
Ginger fresh 1/2 teaspoon / 2g. ....metal
Bocksdorn fruits, goji berry dried 1 table spoon / 8g. ....wood

Cooking instructions:

Soak shiitake mushrooms. Blanch oxtail slices (This removes fat and impurities). Cook in the beef broth for 1-2 hours.
Then add the spring onions, shiitake mushrooms, rice wine, buckthorn fruits and ginger and simmer gently.

9.12 Coconut soup

Forces Qi and blood, is very warming, nourishes Yin, blood and Jing, moisturizes, relaxes, builds up Qi, spreads, gets Qi moving, directs upwards, dissolves stagnation.
Cooking time approx. 20 min
Calories p. portion: 153
6 portions
Allergens: L

Quantity of ingredients

Olive oil 2 table spoons / 20g. .... earth
Leek 1 piece / 200g. ....metal
Onion white 1 small / 40g. ....metal
Basic recipe for a chicken soup (warming) 4 cup / 1000g. ....*
Lime 1/2 juice / 20g. ....wood
Coconut flakes 2 table spoons / 18g. .... earth
Coconut milk 1 cup / 250g. .... earth
Pimento 1 pinch / 0,2g. ....metal
Salt (herbal) 1 pinch / 1g. ....water
Lemongrass 1 table spoon / 8g. ....*

Cooking instructions:

Pour olive oil into a pan, sauté the leek and onion, add the chicken broth, add the lemon grass, simmer for about 15 minutes, add coconut flakes and coconut milk, allspice and chilli, salt with herb salt. Garnish with lemongrass.

9.13 Cod soup with tomatoes

Strengthens kidney Qi, strengthens blood and fluids, promotes urination, forces Qi from spleen and kidney, softens, passes downwardly, scatters and move Qi, moisturizes, reduces cold-evil, softens knots, nourishes liver-Yin.
Cooking time approx. 30 min
Calories p. portion: 176
4 portions
Allergens: DLO

Quantity of ingredients
Basic recipe for a fish soup 2 cup / 450g. ....*
Cod 5/8 lbs - 8oz / 250g. ....water
Onion (shallot) 1 piece / 20g. ....metal
Anise (Common Fennel) 1/2 teaspoon / 1g. .... earth
Ginger fresh 1/2 teaspoon / 1g. ....metal
Olive oil 1 teaspoon / 3g. .... earth
Tomato 1 piece / 50g. ....wood
White wine 1/2 cup / 125g. ....wood
Salt 1 pinch / 0,5g. ....water
Pepper (ground) 1 pinch / 0,2g. ....metal
Parsley 1 table spoon (chopped) / 5g. ....wood

Cooking instructions:
Fry the onion, anise and freshly grated ginger in oil.
Add finely chopped tomatoes and sauté. Add a little wine and fish soup. Simmer gently for 10-15 minutes. Season with salt and pepper; Add the cod pieces and heat gently. Garnish with parsley at the end.

9.14 Cooling rice dish with grapefruit

Lowers lung Qi, nourishes fluids, dissolves mucus, dries out, passes downwardly, warms the stomach and spleen, harmonizes the intestine, forces Qi, reduces moisture, strengthens Qi and Kidney Jing, moisturizes, relaxes, builds up Qi, spreads.
Cooking time approx. 20 min
Calories p. portion: 234
4 portions
Allergens: GHO

Quantity of ingredients

Rice round grain 1 cup / 120g. ....metal
Water 5 cups / 600g. (yes) .... earth
Hazelnuts 2 table spoons / 20g. .... earth
Raisins 2 table spoons / 20g. .... earth
Agave nectar 1 table spoon / 10g. ....*
Salt 1 pinch / 0,2g. ....water
Almond puree 1 table spoon / 10g. .... earth
Grapefruit (Pomelo) 1 piece / 200g. .... fire
Butter organic 2 teaspoons / 20g. .... earth

Cooking instructions:

Preparation on the eve: Pour round grain rice into cold water and cook.
Soak chopped hazelnuts and raisins in some hot water overnight.
In the morning: Stir in a little hot water some agave syrup; add the rice
and heat; add a small pinch of salt, almond paste, chopped grapefruit, the
soaked chopped hazelnuts and raisins and mix; Serve with a small piece
of butter.

9.15 Cous-Cous with date, coco and almondpuree

Forces Yin.
Cooking time approx. 10 min
Calories p. portion: 484
3 portions
Allergens: AHO

Quantity of ingredients

Couscous 1 1/2 cups / 240g. ....wood
Water 4 cups / 400g. (yes) .... earth
Dates dried 6 pieces / 20g. .... earth
Coconut flakes 2 table spoons / 30g. .... earth
Almond puree 2 table spoons / 20g. .... earth
Olive oil 2 teaspoons / 20g. .... earth
Apple (sweet) 1 piece grated / 120g. .... earth
Vanilla 1 knife tip / 0,2g. ....*

Cooking instructions:

Put couscous and olive oil in a large bowl and pour boiling water over
them. Let it swell for 10 minutes. Crush dates and grate apple. Loosen up
cous-cous with a fork. Mix in dates, coconut flakes, apple and almond
paste.
Sweet to taste. Spices and flavors: vanilla, little chili

Winter variation: pear,
Summer variation: apricot, nectarine

9.16 Italian champignon rice

Nourishes blood, moisturizes, relaxes, builds up Qi, spreads, warms the stomach and spleen, harmonizes the intestine, forces Qi, reduces moisture, directs upwards, moisturizes, relaxes, builds up Qi, spreads.
Cooking time approx. 25 min
Calories p. portion: 256
4 portions
Allergens: G

Quantity of ingredients
Rice round grain 1 1/2 cups / 240g. ....metal
Water 2 cup / 450g. (yes) .... earth
Pepper (ground) 1 pinch / 0,2g. ....metal
Salt 1 pinch / 0,5g. ....water
Lemon juice 1 dash / 2g. ....wood
Champignon 5/8 lbs - 8oz / 250g. .... earth
Pepper powder (hot) 1 pinch / 0,2g. .... fire
Olive oil 1 teaspoon / 3g. .... earth
Chives 1 teaspoon / 5g. ....metal
Parmesan 2 table spoons / 20g. .... earth

Cooking instructions:
Put the round grain rice in cold water 1:6 and cook.
Add ground pepper, salt, plenty of lemon juice, rose paprika, a little olive oil or butter and mix well.
Carefully add in mushrooms, chives or the green parts of the spring onion, and carefully add in some grated Parmesan cheese.
Goes well with vegetables and tofu dishes, tomato sauce dishes.

9.17 Melanzani with olive oil and turmeric

Cools and moves blood, reduces external and internal wind, reduces internal heat, nourishes liver-Yin, cools heat, produces humors, moisturizes, relaxes, builds up Qi, spreads.
Cooking time approx. 30 min
Calories p. portion: 432
2 portions
Allergens: A

Quantity of ingredients

Aubergine 2 pieces / 300g. .... earth
Olive oil 4 table spoons / 60g. .... earth
Tomato 4 pieces / 200g. .... wood
Turmeric (yellow root) 1/2 teaspoon / 1g. ....*
Ground 1 pinch / 1g. .... earth
Salt 1 pinch / 1g. .... water
White bread (wheat bread) 4 slices / 80g. .... wood

Cooking instructions:
Cut the melanzani into slices and spread them with the tomatoes on a baking tray. Sprinkle with olive oil and then with turmeric, caraway and salt. Bake them in the tube 20 min.
Serve with the white bread.

9.18 Milk rice with berry juice

Nourishes fluids, moisturises dryness, weakness, produces humors, moisturizes intestines, cools inner heat, forces essence, warms the stomach and spleen, harmonizes the intestine, forces Qi, reduces moisture.
Cooking time approx. 25 min
Calories p. portion: 135
1 portions
Allergens: G

Quantity of ingredients

Raspberry 2 table spoons / 30g. .... wood
Cow's milk (1.5% fat) 3/4 cup - 6 oz / 200g. ....*
Rice mash 2 table spoons / 10g. .... metal

Cooking instructions:
Thaw the frozen raspberries and then pass through a sieve. Mix half of the milk with the rice bran. Heat till it boils in a small saucepan and simmer over low heat while stirring for about 3 minutes. Remove the saucepan from the heat and gradually add the remaining milk and raspberry juice. Add the liquid to the bottle and shake vigorously. Depending on the season and preferences, add with fruit juices, glucose and from the 8th month, with honey or sugar cane granules.

9.19 Millet with egg and butter

Forces blood, Yin and Jing, nourishes Yin, moisturizes in case of internal dryness, forces blood, forces spleen, calms nerves and stomach, strengthens spleen and kidney, diuretic, strengthens Qi and kidney Jing, moisturizes, relaxes, builds up Qi, spreads.
Cooking time approx. 25 min
Calories p. portion: 338
2 portions
Allergens: CG

Quantity of ingredients
Millet 1 cup / 100g. .... earth
Ginger fresh 1/2 teaspoon / 1g. ....metal
Salt 1 pinch / 0,5g. ....water
Parsley 2 table spoons / 16g. ....wood
Pepper powder (hot) 1 pinch / 1g. .... fire
Chicken egg 2 pieces / 100g. .... earth
Butter organic 2 table spoons / 20g. .... earth
Nutmeg 1 pinch / 0,2g. ....metal
Water 1 1/2 cups / 200g. (yes)... earth

Cooking instructions:
Simmer the millet with the ginger and nutmeg in the water for 5 min. and let it swell for another 30 min.
Cook and peel 1 soft egg per person; pile up the millet on plates and place 1 egg each in a hollow in the millet mountain; Put butterflakes over it. Sprinkle with chopped parsley and the rose paprika.

9.20 Polenta with peach

Strengthens blood and fluids, brings blood into motion, builds up Qi, spreads, strengthens stomach Qi, diuretic, moisturizes, relaxes, builds up Qi, spreads, warms the stomach and spleen, promotes blood circulation and conduction flow, relieves cold-sickness and pain.
Cooking time approx. 20 min
Calories p. portion: 197
3 portions

Quantity of ingredients
Water 1 1/2 cups / 240g. (yes)... earth
Corn Grease (Polenta) 1 cup / 120g. .... earth
Peaches 2-3 pieces / 400g. .... earth
Vanilla pod 1 pinch / 1g. .... *

Cinnamon ground 1 pinch / 1g. ....*

Cooking instructions:
Pour the polenta into a pan of hot water with constant stirring until the polenta has the desired consistency. Pull the
 polenta from the fire and let it soak for 10 minutes.

Wash fresh peaches and cut into quarters. Pour into the finished polenta the peaches, add the vanilla and add Chili
 to taste, stir and let it go for 3 minutes.

Winter varieties: Pickled fruit, pear, apples

9.21 Polenta with ratatouille

Strengthens stomach Qi, diuretic, moisturizes, relaxes, builds up Qi, spreads, nourishes liver-Yin, cools heat, produces humors, cools and moves blood, reduces external and internal wind, reduces internal heat.
Cooking time approx. 30 min
Calories p. portion: 226
4 portions
Allergens: G

Quantity of ingredients
Corn Grease (Polenta) 1 cup / 120g. .... earth
Water 1 1/2 cups / 240g. (yes).. earth
Aubergine 1 piece (large) / 200g. .... earth
Zucchini 2 pieces / 500g. .... earth
Onion white 2 pieces / 120g. ....metal
Tomato 2 pieces (blended) / 200g. .... wood
Olive oil 2 table spoons / 20g. .... earth
Salt 1 pinch / 0,5g. ....water
Parsley 1 table spoon (chopped) / 8g. .... wood
Thyme 1/2 teaspoon / 1g. ....*
Onion (spring onion) 2 table spoons (chopped) / 12g. ....metal
Basil 4 leaves / 2g. ....metal
Parmesan 2 table spoons / 20g. .... earth

Cooking instructions:
Use double the amount of water to polenta, add salt and oil and heat till it boils. Stir in polenta, stirring constantly. Take off the fire and let it swell for 20 minutes. Meanwhile, cut the onion, fry in a saucepan with hot oil. Add the diced zucchini, tomatoes and melanzani and simmer for about 20

minutes. Add basil, thyme, salt.
Coat baking tray with oil, apply polenta evenly and wait until it gets stronger.
Add the cooked ratatouille to polenta, portion and then put in the oven for a few minutes (possibly with grated parmesan).
Sprinkle with fresh parsley and finely chopped spring onion.
The valuable tip: The Polenta sections are ideal for on the go.

9.22 Quick flakes with compote or jam

Forces Qi, dries out, passes downwardly, strengthens middle heater, moisturizes, relaxes, builds up Qi, spreads, strengthens kidney Qi, essence and brain, forces kidney, warms the middle.
Cooking time approx. 5 min
Calories p. portion: 189
2 portions
Allergens: H

Quantity of ingredients
Quinoa 5-7 table spoons / 50g. .... fire
Water 1 cup / 250g. (yes) .... earth
Compote (fruits of the season) 1 cup / 100g. ....*
Walnuts 1 table spoon (grated) / 8g. .... earth
Olive oil 1 table spoon / 10g. .... earth
Honey 2 table spoons / 20g. .... earth
Vanilla 1 pinch / 0,2g. ....*
Anise (Common Fennel) 1 pinch / 0,2g. .... earth
Cardamom 1 pinch / 0,2g. ....*

Cooking instructions:
Put the quinoa flakes in a pan and add water. Boil for 3-5 minutes, pull from the fire, add nuts and compote. Add a dash of oil. Sweeten as needed with honey, whole cane sugar or agave syrup.

Spices and aromas: vanilla, anise, fennel or coriander, cardamom, a little chili.

Winter: apple compote, pear compote, fruit jam.
Summer: plum compote, apricot compote.

9.23 Quinoa with peach

Strengthens blood and fluids, brings blood into motion, builds up Qi, spreads, forces Qi, dries out, passes downwardly, strengthens middle heater, moisturizes.
Cooking time approx. 20 min
Calories p. portion: 248
2 portions

Quantity of ingredients
Quinoa 1 cup / 100g. .... fire
Water 1 1/2 cups / 240g. (yes).. earth
Honey 2 teaspoons / 4g. .... earth
Peaches 2 pieces / 240g. .... earth
Linseed oil 2 teaspoons / 4g. .... earth
Lemon Balm (fresh) 1 teaspoon (chopped) / 1g. ....metal
Cinnamon ground 1 pinch / 0,2g. ....*
Vanilla 1 pinch / 0,2g. ....*

Cooking instructions:
In the evening: Put quinoa in hot water and boil soft, covered 15 to 20 minutes.
In the morning: Warm up quinoa with 1 tablespoon water.
Steam lightly Peaches in a saucepan or add them fresh. Decorate with fresh lemon balm.

Summer: nectarines, apricots
Winter: Pickled fruit, pear, apples

9.24 Radish with horseradish

Slightly refreshing and moisturizing, dissolves stagnation, nourishes blood and liver, harmonizes liver and spleen, forces eyesight, preserves the fluids, contracts, nourishes the lungs and spleen, distributes mucus, dissolves mucus, dissolves stagnation, directs upwards.
Cooking time approx. 30 min
Calories p. portion: 196
2 portions
Allergens: GNO

Quantity of ingredients

Butter organic 1 table spoon / 8g. .... earth
Radish (white, green, purple-red) 1/2 piece / 50g. .... metal
Water 2 table spoons / 10g. (yes).. earth
Lemon juice 2 table spoons / 20g. .... wood
White wine 2 table spoons / 20g. .... wood
Pepper powder (hot) 1 pinch / 0,2g. .... fire
Sesame oil 1 teaspoon / 3g. .... earth
Radish horseradish 2 table spoons / 20g. .... metal
Salt 1 pinch / 0,5g. .... water
Parsley 1 Bunch (chopped) / 80g. .... wood
Rice long grain rice 1/2 cup / 60g. .... metal
Water 3 cups / 300g. (yes) .... earth
Salt 1 pinch / 0,5g. .... water

Cooking instructions:
In a hot pan melt the butter, sautéed into stripes cut radish. Add cold water, lemon juice, white wine, a pinch of rose paprika and stir in the sesame oil; with 2 - 3 tablespoons fresh grated horseradish (alternatively 1 teaspoon from the glass), salt to taste; Sprinkle with chopped parsley.

Place the rice with the water, salt and cook for about 15 minutes.

9.25 Red lentils with avocado and radish

Nutritious and moisturizing builds up Qi and fluids, drives sweat, reduces blood fat, stimulates, dissolves stagnation.
Cooking time approx. 20 min
Calories p. portion: 269
3 portions
Allergens: N

Quantity of ingredients

Ginger fresh 2 slices / 2g. .... metal
Water 1 1/2 cups / 200g. (yes)... earth
Lentils red 1 cup peeled / 100g. .... water
Wakame 1 inch / 1g. .... water
Salt 1 pinch / 0,5g. .... water
Lemon juice 1 dash / 1g. .... wood
Curcuma 1 pinch / 0,3g. .... *
Avocado 1 piece / 300g. .... earth
Pepper (ground) 1 pinch / 0,2g. .... metal
Pepper powder (hot) 1 pinch / 0,2g. .... fire

Sesame oil 1 dash / 1g. .... earth
Radish (white, green, purple-red) 1 cup / 100g. ....metal

Cooking instructions:
Put in a pot with water, some chopped ginger, peeled red lentils, a piece of wakame or a small amount of hijiki and simmer until the lentils are soft. Season with salt, lemon juice and turmeric.

Meanwhile: place half an avocado per serving on one-third of the plate: add ground pepper, a pinch of salt, a little lemon juice, a pinch of sweet pepper and a little sesame oil.

Put the grated radish on the second plate third.

Fill the lentil dish into the last third of the plate.
Variant: Use radish slices instead of radishes.

9.26 Semolina mash with grape puree

Nourishes fluids, moisturizes dryness, produces humors, moisturizes intestines, reduces liver Yin-Xu, soothes stomach.
Cooking time approx. 10 min
Calories p. portion: 204
1 portions
Allergens: AG

Quantity of ingredients
Grapes white 6 pieces / 15g. .... earth
Cow's milk (1.5% fat) 3/4 cup - 6 oz / 200g. ....*
Wheat semolina for children 2 table spoons / 30g. ....wood

Cooking instructions:
Wash the grapes, cut in half, remove the peel and remove the seeds. Finely chop the pulp, collecting the juice. Heat half of the milk. Add the semolina (not whole wheat), heat till it boils and simmer over low heat with stirring in about 3 minutes. Remove the pot from the cooking area and gradually add the remaining milk and the grape marc. You can easily sweeten semolina pudding with fruit purée or fruit juice.

9.27 Spelled-grid porridge with berries of the season

Nourishes fluids, moisturises dryness, produces humors, moisturizes intestines, cools inner heat, preserves the fluids, contracts, forces middle, nourishes heart and liver-blood, preserves the fluids, contracts.
Cooking time approx. 15 min
Calories p. portion: 244
2 portions
Allergens: AGH

Quantity of ingredients
Cow's milk (1.5% fat) 1/2 cup / 125g. .... *
Water 1/2 cup / 125g. (yes) .... earth
Spelled semolina 5 table spoons / 50g. .... wood
Butter organic 2 teaspoons / 20g. .... earth
Berries of the season 1/4 lbs - 4oz / 100g. .... wood
Honey 1-2 teaspoons / 5g. .... earth
Almond 1-2 teaspoons / 5g. .... earth
Peppermint 3-4 leaves / 2g. .... metal
Cinnamon ground 1 pinch / 0,5g. .... *
Vanilla 1 pinch / 0,2g. .... *
Cocoa 1 pinch / 0,5g. .... fire
Coconut grated 1 table spoon / 10g. .... earth

Cooking instructions:
Stir in spelled semolina in cold water and boil slowly over medium heat. After boiling, remove from the heat and let simmer for a few minutes. Depending on the desired consistency, some water may have to be added. Stir in the butter and fine grated nuts in the mash and raspberries. Serve with honey or whole-grain sugar as desired.
Spices and aromas: fresh mint, cinnamon or vanilla, cocoa, coconut

Summer: raspberries, blueberries, strawberries

9.28 Summer Salad

Nourishes liver-Yin, cools heat, dissolves mucus, forces Xu-conditions, passes downwardly, brings blood into motion.
Cooking time approx. 10 min
Calories p. portion: 281
1 portions
Allergens: GMNO

Quantity of ingredients

Rucola Handful / 15g. .... fire
Radicchio 1 head / 30g. .... fire
Tomato 15 pieces (diced) / 100g. .... wood
Olive oil 1 table spoon / 10g. .... earth
Olives 2 table spoons / 16g. .... fire
Vinegar Aceto Balsamico 1 table spoon / 10g. .... wood
Mustard medium hot 2 teaspoons / 5g. .... metal
Sesame paste (Tahini) 1 teaspoon / 2g. .... earth
Parmesan 2 table spoons / 20g. .... earth
Salt 1 pinch / 0,5g. .... water
Pepper (ground) 1 pinch / 0,2g. .... metal
Rosemary 2 teaspoons / 3g. .... fire

Cooking instructions:
Wash the salad, pluck it small and arrange it in a bowl.

Sauce: Put the oil, the balsamic vinegar, the mustard and the tahini in a glass with a lid and shake well. Season the dressing with salt and pepper. Mix the salad with the salad dressing and the olives, sprinkle with parmesan and finally with rosemary.

9.29 Wild garlic pesto

Gets Qi moving, detoxifies, builds up blood, moisturizes the lungs and large intestine.
Cooking time approx. 10 min
Calories p. portion: 796
2 portions
Allergens: G

Quantity of ingredients

Wild garlic (garlic spinach) 1/4 lbs - 4oz / 125g. .... metal
Parmesan 1 oz / 30g. .... earth
Pine nuts 1/8 lbs - 2oz / 50g. .... earth
Olive oil 1/4 lbs - 4oz / 125g. .... earth
Salt 1 pinch / 1g. .... water
Pepper (ground) 1 pinch / 0,3g. .... metal

Cooking instructions:
Fresh wild garlic: Wash the wild garlic leaves and dry them carefully. Cut the wild garlic leaves into fine strips. Dried wild garlic: Leave approx. 80g in 40g of water for 10 minutes.

Carefully roast the pine nuts. The pine nuts should be light brown after roasting. Cut the pine nuts very finely with a large knife or rub them with a nut mill. Pick up some of the seeds to decorate the pesto later.
Place all ingredients in a tall container and chop and mix with a blender. Put the pesto in a bowl or in a glass.
In the fridge, the pesto lasts a while (days to weeks) and is therefore a way to preserve bear's garlic.
You can eat wild garlic pesto as sauce with spaghetti, but it also tastes great with potatoes or bread.

10 Herbs and their effects

10.1 Basil

thermal effect: warm
taste:spicy, bitter
Dries out, leads down. Tonifies Yang and Qi, dissolves mucus-cold, eliminates wind-cold.
It has a beneficial effect on flatulence and nausea, relaxing and soothing. Good to fight emphysema, bronchitis, whooping cough, high blood pressure, headache, mouth odor, warts, hiccup, gout, migraine.

10.2 Chives

thermal effect: warm
taste:spicy
Directs upward. Tonifies blood, kidney Yang and Qi. Dissolves moisture. Bactericide, prevents cancer, strengthens gastric juice production, promotes digestion and blood circulation, promotes growth, triggers stagnation.

10.3 Lily bulbs

thermal effect: cool
taste:sweet, bitter
Tonifies Yin, soothes Shen / Spirit. Moisturizes the lungs, clears heat and stops coughing.
Calms nerves, good to fight scaly skin. The onions and the petals are added to ointments in the Orient, which can heal muscles and tendons. White lily (astringent).

10.4 Oregano fresh

thermal effect: warm
taste:bitter
Dries out, directs down, regulates and moves Qi, eliminates wind-cold, soothes Shen / Spirit, suppresses inner wind, warms inside, eliminates wind-cold / heat-wetness, moves blood, dissolves slime-cold.
It has an anti-digestive, calming and nerve-strengthening effect, helps to fight cramping stomach and intestinal disorders. The ingredient Carvacrol has an anti-inflammatory effect.

10.5 Parsley

thermal effect: warm
taste:bitter
Nourishes blood and liver, harmonizes liver and spleen, strengthens eyesight, preserves juices, contracts. Dissolves moisture and warms Yang.
Stimulates liver function, detoxifies. Forces urinating. Relieves flatulence.
Digestive and menstrual stimulating, birth-accelerating, memory-enhancing, blood-purifying, skin-smoothing.

10.6 Peppermint

thermal effect: cool
taste:spicy, bitter
Cools heat, expels mucus, dissipates wind-cold and wind-heat, moves stomach qi, releases congestion, tonifies, regulates and moves qi.
Relaxes, frees the lungs and the nose (inhale), regulates the cycle.
Stimulates bile flow and bile production, antispasmodic in gastrointestinal disorders, antimicrobial and antiviral.

10.7 Rosemary

thermal effect: warm
taste:bitter
Dries out, leads down. Strengthens the heart, lungs and spleen qi, strengthens liver blood. Strengthens heart-Yin.
Expels spleen heat / cold moisture. Strengthens spleen and kidney yang.
Promotes digestion, relieves bloating, strengthens lung, spleen and kidney. Affects the circulation and nerves.
Appetizing. Baths help to fight circulatory disorders as well as with gout and rheumatism.

10.8 King Solomon's-seal

thermal effect: neutral
taste:sweet, bitter
Tonifies Yin and Qi, astringent, tonifies blood, eliminates wind-cold / heat-wetness.
Used to repair wounds or damaged tissue. Good to fight dry cough, earlier also tuberculosis and dysentery, as well as diarrhea and hemorrhoids.

10.9 Yam root, yam root tuber

thermal effect: neutral
taste:sweet
Tonifies Yin, Yang and Qi, reduces inner wind, dissolves wetness, warms Yang.
Solves cramps (in the gastrointestinal tract). Digestive through increased bile production. Anti-inflammatory in rheumatic diseases.
Mucolytic agent for coughing. Relief of menopausal symptoms.

10.10   Lemongrass

thermal effect: taste:
Diverting, calming.
Reduction of flatulence, antimicrobial, appetizing. Prevention of influenza.
Good to fight infections in the mouth and throat.

10.11   Lemon Balm (fresh)

thermal effect: cool
taste:sour
Soothes Shen / Spirit, regulates and moves Qi, eliminates heat caused by Yin deficiency, tones Qi.
Stimulating, antibacterial, encouraging, relaxing, antispasmodic, cooling, antipyretic, analgesic, sweat-inducing, virus-inhibiting. Good for colds, fever, flu, cough, bronchitis, asthma, loss of appetite, bloating, heartburn.

11 Basics of Nutrition

The basic principles of nutrition described herein are general recommendations. They are not aimed at a specific form of therapy. Recommendations concerning a therapy have priority.

11.1 Nutrition

Regular meals in a relaxed atmosphere. A warm breakfast is considered a good start into the day.
The main meals ought to be taken for lunch – supper in the early evening. Pay attention to feeling hungry or sated: don't eat too much nor remain hungry is the rule
Prepare the meals freshly from natural, regional products. Frozen, heat-conserved, industrially prepared or foodstuffs cooked in the microwave oven are rejected.
Choice of foodstuffs according to the season: more cooling food in summer, more warming food in winter.
Eat cooked food at least twice a day. Food and drinks ought to be lukewarm, never ice-cold or hot.
Raw vegetables, briefly cooked vegetables, freshly squeezed juices and mineral water are not recommended. Milk and dairy products are only included in the diet if they don't cause problems. Don't use therapeutic recipes over a longer period without consulting your doctor or therapist.

Varied food
Enjoy the diversity of foodstuffs. Characteristics of a balanced nutrition are variety, suitable combination and a balanced quantity of rich and low energy foodstuffs (on one hand avoiding undersupply with essential nutrients and on the other hand to take to many undesirable substances).

A lot of Cereal Products - and Potatoes
Bread, pasta, rice, cereal flakes (best wholemeal) as well as potatoes contain almost no fat, but many vitamins, mineral nutrients, trace elements, roughage and secondary plant substances. These foodstuffs ought to be taken with low-fat side dishes.

Vegetables and Fruit – „Take Five" every day ... 5 portions of vegetables and fruit a day, as fresh as possible, briefly cooked, or maybe one portion as a juice – ideal as a side dish to every meal as well as snack between meals: Thus a lot of vitamins, mineral nutrients as well as roughage and secondary plant substances

Daily milk and dairy products
Milk and Dairy Products every Day, once or twice per Week Fish; meat, sausages as well as eggs moderately. These foodstuffs contain valuable nutrients like calcium in the milk, iodine selenium and omega-3 fat acids in saltwater fish. Meat is favorable due to its high content of disposable iron and the vitamins B1, B6 and B12. Quantities of 300 – 600 g meat and sausage per week are sufficient. Prefer low-fat products, especially in meat- and dairy products.

Low-fat and fatty Foodstuffs
Fat supplies us with essential fat acids and fatty foodstuffs contain also fat-soluble vitamins. Fat is high in energy; therefore much fat in the food may cause overweight, possibly also cancer. Too many saturated fat acids may further a tendency for cardio-vascular diseases in the long term. Prefer vegetable oils and fats (e.g. rapeseed-, olive-, soya-oils and solid fats produced therefrom). Beware of invisible fat in meat- and dairy products, pastry and sweets as well as in fast-food and convenience foods. 70 – 90 g fat per day is sufficient.

Moderately Sugar and Salt
Take sugar and foods/drinks containing various kinds of sugar (e.g. glucose syrup) only occasionally. Use herbs and spices as well as a little salt creatively. Prefer salt containing iodine.

Plenty of Liquids
Water is absolutely essential. Drink 1-2 l liquids every day. Prefer water (with or without gas) and other low-calorie drinks. Alcoholic drinks should not be taken.

Tasty Dishes, carefully cooked
Cook the meals with as low temperatures and as short as possible, using little water and fat – this preserves the original taste, keeps the nutrients intact and prevents the production of harmful compounds.

Take time and enjoy the food
Take your Time and enjoy your Food
Eating consciously helps to eat right. The eye enjoys food, too. It's fun, invites to enjoy varied dishes and stimulates the feeling of satiety.

Watch your Weight and stay in Motion
A balanced diet and a lot of exercise and sport (30 – 60 min/day) are a healthy combination. The right weight furthers well-being and health. Thermals, directional effectiveness, digestive power

There are various criteria for judging the effectiveness of herbs and foodstuffs.

The use of certain herbs and ingredients is based on observations of the effects on the body which these foodstuffs, herbs and spices show after having eaten them. The medical science has developed following system: Every ingredient or herb has a directional effectiveness. Furthermore, there are herbs which have a special effect on certain organs.

The basic condition for a healthy metabolism is to obtain sufficient energy from food and that the digestive process doesn't use too much energy. An easily digestible meal makes content and sated, doesn't cause flatulence and fatigue after the meal. The perfect spices increase the healthiness of our meals. Very often, just small doses of herbs and spices will suffice. They are not used to make us sated, but to help our digestive organs to digest the food.

11.2 Recipes

The recipes list the ingredients to be used and the cooking instructions show how the dish is prepared. The list of ingredients shows the concerned quantities as well as the relevance for the therapy. If you find „less than mentioned", try to comply or find an alternative from the „list of recommended foodstuffs". Mostly it shall result just in a small change of taste when you simply avoid this ingredient.

Mild cooking methods: boiling, stewing, poaching, steaming
Strong cooking methods: barbecuing, roasting, frying, smoking
Balanced cooking methods: deep-frying, baking brick
Deep-freezing and warming in the microwave oven should be avoided (denaturalization).

11.3 Foodstuffs

Foodstuffs have an effect on body and soul like medicinal herbs, only a very much milder one. Dietary advice is mainly based on regional foodstuffs. The knowledge about the effects of each foodstuff and the knowledge, when which foodstuff shall be used, is based on the orthodox school of medicine. Use ecologic-organic products, if possible. As everything should be cooked for a long time due to a better digestability and very rarely eaten raw, the food agrees with everyone.

The classification of the foodstuffs according to their effect on the body is the basis in order to achieve a harmonious status of health.

Dietary advisors do not recommend certain foodstuffs for everyone. The individual diet is tailor-made for the individual constitution.

Buy only fresh and ripe fruit and vegetables. You ought to leave unripe fruit and vegetables and such with brown spots and wilted leaves behind in the market. In this case take deep-frozen goods (never ready-to-serve dishes!). Fruit and vegetables are deep-frozen immediately after harvesting and often contain more vitamins and minerals than the goods from the vegetable shelf. Whereas conserved or tinned goods contain very much less biological substances. Also, salt, sugar and others are mostly added to the latter. Never leave the foodstuffs in the water after washing them to avoid that many vital substances get drowned. Clean salads, fruit and vegetables immediately before serving.

Please make sure of the hygienic processing of foodstuffs. Clean your salads, fruit and vegetables carefully. When cooking with meat, prepare all ingredients first and then process the meat products. Clean the worktop and tools very carefully. Wooden surfaces ought to be treated with a mild disinfectant regularly in order to reduce germination.
Store fruit and vegetables separately, if possible. Harvested fruit and vegetables are still alive and emit e.g. ethylene gas, which makes other products ripen and age faster. Keep meat and fish in the closed packaging or store them in the fridge in closed containers.

11.4 Herbs

There are some basic rules for storing medicinal herbs. On principle, herbs must be protected from direct sunlight, humidity and heat.

Containers for the storage of herbs may be glasses, ceramic jars and even plastic containers. However, plastic is a rather unsuitable material and should only be a short-term solution. In case of glass containers, use a dark material.

Medicinal herbs cannot be kept for any long period. The shelf life of herbs is limited. However, it can be prolonged with suitable storage. The place should be dark, rather cool and absolutely dry. A wooden medicine cabinet, placed not directly next to a source of heat, would be ideal. Never buy large quantities of herbs so as not to have to throw them away. Label the container with the name of the herb and the date of harvesting or processing.

12 Other dietic-books

The following syndromes of dietetics, TCM or for a therapy supplement for cancer are available.

Dietetics
E001. Nutrition of the infant - baby food
E002. Nutrition during lactation
E003. Nutrition in old age
E004. Nutrition of children and adolescents
E005. Nutrition of athletes
E006. Light weight
E007. Pregnancy
E008. Full food

Protein and electrolyte - kidneys
E009. (hemodialysis) dialysis treatment
E010. Acute renal failure
E011. Chronic renal insufficiency
E012. Nephrotic syndrome
E013. Kidney stones (nephrolithiasis)

Gastrointestinal tract - pancreas
E014. Acute pancreatitis (inflammation of the pancreas)
E015. Chronic pancreatitis (inflammation of the pancreas)

Gastrointestinal tract - small intestine and large intestine
E016. Acute obstipation (constipation)
E017. Chronic obstipation (constipation)
E018. Colon irritabile
E019. Diverticulitis
E020. Acquired lactose intolerance (lactose malabsorption)
E021. Fructose malabsorption
E022. Glutensensitive enteropathy (celiac disease)
E023. Colectomy
E024. Short Bowel Syndrome

Gastrointestinal tract - liver, gallbladder, bile ducts
E025. Acute and chronic hepatitis (inflammation of the liver)
E026. Cholelithiasis (bile stones)
E027. fatty liver
E028. cirrhosis

Gastrointestinal tract - Stomach and duodenal intestine
E029. Acute gastritis
E030. Chronic gastritis
E031. Stomach bleeding
E032. Ulcus ventriculi and duodenal ulcer
E033. Condition after gastric surgery

Gastrointestinal tract - oral cavity and esophagus
E034. Stomatitis
E035. Esophageal carcinoma (esophageal cancer)
E036. Refluosophagitis (heartburn)

Special diseases
E037. Phenylketonuria (PKU)
E038. Rheumatic joint diseases

Metabolism
E039. Obesity (overweight)
E040. Diabetes mellitus
E041. Eating disorders (underweight)

Fat metabolism
E042. Hypercholesterolaemia (increased cholesterol level)
E043. Hepatic Encephalopathy

Heart and circulation
E044. Arteriosclerosis (arterial calcification)
E045. Heart insufficiency
E046. Hypertension
E047. Hyperuricaemia and gout

Changed nutrient requirements
E048. In case of fever
E049. For malignant diseases
E050. After burns
E051. Radiation and chemotherapy

CANCER
E100. Pancreatic cancer
E101. Bladder cancer
E102. Blood cancer (leukemia)
E103. Breast cancer
E104. Colorectal cancer
E105. Gastric cancer
E106. Kidney cancer
E107. Esophageal cancer

TCM
E200. Bladder - moisture heat in the bladder
E201. Bladder - moisture and cold in the bladder
E202. Bladder - emptiness and cold in the bladder
E203. Large intestine - external cold affects the large intestine
E204. Large intestine - moisture heat in the large intestine
E205. Large intestine - heat blocks the intestine II acute
E206. Large intestine - dryness of the colon
E207. Large intestine - Yang deficiency (cold)
E208. Heart - Blood insufficiency
E209. Heart - Blood stagnation
E210. Heart - Fire
E211. Heart - Hot mucus clogs the heart pores

E212. Heart - Cold mucus clogs the heart pores
E213. Heart - Qi deficiency
E214. Heart - Yang deficiency
E215. Heart - Yin deficiency
E216. Liver - Ascending Liver Yang
E217. Liver - Blood deficiency
E218. Liver - Blood stagnation
E219. Liver - Moisture heat in liver and gall bladder
E220. Liver - Fire
E221. Liver - Gall bladder Qi-Empty
E222. Liver - Cold in the liver meridian
E223. Liver - Qi stagnation
E224. Liver - Wind
E225. Liver - Wind with ascending liver Yang
E226. Liver - Wind with blood anemic
E227. Liver - Wind with extreme heat
E228. Lung - Qi deficiency
E229. Lung - Mucus-moisture in the lungs
E230. Lung - Mucus-heat in the lungs
E231. Lung - Mucus-cold in the lungs
E232. Lung - Dryness of the lungs
E233. Lung - Wind-heat attacks the lungs
E234. Lung - Wind-cold affects the lungs
E235. Lung - Yin deficiency
E236. Stomach - Bloodstagnation
E237. Stomach - Fire
E238. Stomach - Cold with liquid
E239. Stomach - Nutrition stagnation
E240. Stomach - Qi deficiency
E241. Stomach - Rebellious Qi
E242. Stomach - Yin Emptiness
E243. Spleen - Heat and moisture attack the spleen
E244. Spleen - Coldness and moisture affects the spleen
E245. Spleen - Qi deficiency
E246. Spleen - Qi deficiency + Declining spleen Qi
E247. Spleen - Qi deficiency + spleen does not control the blood
E248. Spleen - Yang deficiency
E249. Kidney - Heart and kidney no longer communicate
E250. Kidney - Jing deficiency
E251. Kidney - Kidneys cannot receive the Qi
E252. Kidney - Qi is not stable
E253. Kidney - Yang deficiency
E254. Kidney - Yin deficiency

For further information visit di-book.com.